A Polished and Unpolished Woman

Adeline Mucci

Gotham Books

30 N Gould St.
Ste. 20820, Sheridan, WY 82801
https://gothambooksinc.com/

Phone: 1 (307) 464-7800

© 2024 *Adeline Mucci*. All rights reserved.

No part of this book may be reproduced, stored in a retrieval system, or transmitted by any means without the written permission of the author.

Published by Gotham Books (December 4, 2024)

ISBN: 979-8-3305-8405-5 (P)
ISBN: 979-8-3305-8406-2 (E)

Because of the dynamic nature of the Internet, any web addresses or links contained in this book may have changed since publication and may no longer be valid.

The views expressed in this work are solely those of the author and do not necessarily reflect the views of the publisher, and the publisher hereby disclaims any responsibility for them.

Table of Contents

Acknowledgements
- Acknowledging the Support of Family and Friends

Dedication
- Dedication to God for Guiding My Journey

Introduction
- Life's Unexpected Challenges and Opportunities
- The Role of a Public Safety Officer
- The Unfulfilled Yearning
- The Students' Inspiration
- Embracing Change in Late 50s
- Overcoming Challenges and Office Politics
- Lessons of Perseverance and Growth

Chapter 1: The Beginning
- Introduction
- Immigrating to the United States
- Raising a Family as a Single Parent
- Joining the Local Community College as a Public Safety Officer
- Daily Duties and Fulfillment in the Role
- The Source of Inspiration: The Students
- The Unexpected Catalyst for Change

Chapter 2: Academic Pursuit
- Enrolling in a Master's Program
- Navigating the Enrollment Process
- Juggling Roles: Public Safety Officer and Graduate Student
- The Importance of a Support System
- Lessons in Resilience and Time Management
- The Significance of Family Support

Chapter 3: The Role of Office Politics
- Encountering Office Politics
- The Incident with a Colleague: Judged as 'Unpolished'
- Reflection on the Impact of Office Politics
- Navigating Restructuring
- Turning Adversity into Opportunity for Growth
- The Importance of Resilience and Self-Reflection

Chapter 4: Lessons from a Colleague
- The Arrival of a New Colleague
- Collaborating as Advisors
- The Impact of Office Politics on Career Trajectories
- The Harsh Reality of Merit vs. Personal Bias
- Commitment to Fairness and Equity in the Workplace

Chapter 5: Personality vs. Qualification
- Navigating Competence vs. Bias in the Workplace
- Handling Situations with Incompetent Leadership
- Advocating for Fairness and Meritocracy
- Leading with Integrity and Fairness
- Principles for Professional Conduct

Chapter 6: Character is Destiny
- The Power of Character in Shaping Destiny
- The Influence of Integrity, Empathy, and Perseverance
- Leadership and Its Impact on Organizational Culture
- The Long-term Consequences of Character in Professional Life
- Creating an Environment of Integrity and Fairness

Chapter 7: Lessons Learned
- Personal Growth: Resilience, Adaptability, and Self-Reflection
- Professional Growth: Collaboration, Leadership, and Student-Centered Approach
- Reflections on Office Politics: Integrity, Resilience, and Advocacy

Chapter 8: The Rewards of Perseverance
- A Student's Letter: The Transformative Influence of Educators
- Awards and Recognition: Affirmation of Dedication and Achievement
- Conclusion: A Journey Defined by Challenges, Growth, and Fulfillment
- Student Testimonials: Reflections of Impact and Inspiration
- Looking Ahead: Future Aspirations and Next Steps
- Final Reflections: Embracing Challenges as Pathways to Growth

Acknowledgements

I wish to express my heartfelt gratitude to my family, beginning with my three beloved adult children: my son, Mario Bellevue; my first-born daughter, Marline Bellevue; my second daughter, Christina Remy; and my supportive son-in-law, Marc Duthely. I am also deeply grateful for my three wonderful granddaughters, Mila, Robyn, and Noelle Duthely, whose joy and love bring so much light into my life.

A special thanks to Valerie Hector, one of the most dedicated individuals I have ever known. From the moment I embarked on my graduate journey, Valerie stood by my side, providing unwavering support and guidance through every challenge. Her encouragement has been instrumental, and without her, this book would not have come to fruition.

I also extend my sincere appreciation to Maudelyn Maxineau, who read each chapter with care and always reminded me of my strength and capability.

My gratitude further goes to my dear friend, Monte A. Devendittis, who generously took time from his busy life to review my entire book, assuring me throughout the process that I had what it takes to see this journey through.

To each of you, thank you for your invaluable support, love, and belief in me. This book would not exist without you.

Dedication

Dear God,

I wrote this story about my journey from Public Safety Officer to Instructor and Counselor because I know, with all my heart, that You have guided me from the moment I was conceived in my mother's womb.

I am living proof that grace always prevails. Though You never promised that life would be easy, You did promise that You would never leave or forsake me.

Coming to the USA at the age of 15, I know it is no coincidence that I have achieved so much without the support of my mother and father. You gave me the strength and courage to persevere and reach my full potential.

As long as I live, I will continue to serve others, just as You taught in Matthew 20:28: "Just as the Son of Man did not come to be served, but to serve, and to give His life as a ransom for many."

Your joyful daughter,

Adeline Mucci

Introduction

Life often presents us with unexpected challenges and opportunities that shape our paths in ways we never imagined. For over four years, I served as a Public Safety Officer at a local community college, in Nassau County- role that required both diligence and vigilance. While the duties were fulfilling, a part of me remained unfulfilled, yearning for something more. Little did I know, the very students I was entrusted with protecting would become my greatest source of inspiration and motivation. In many ways, they helped me discover my true passion, even more than I was able to help them.

In my late 50s, a time when many contemplate retirement, I found myself at a crossroads. I decided to take a leap of faith and pursue a dream that had long been dormant— earning a master's degree and transitioning into a role where I could make a direct impact on students' lives. The decision to pursue this path was not an easy one. It came with its own set of challenges, as balancing work, studies, and personal responsibilities often felt overwhelming. Moreover, navigating the intricacies of office politics added another layer of complexity to my journey.

This book, *A Polished and Unpolished Woman,* chronicles my transformative journey from Public Safety Officer to Instructor and Counselor at a local community college, in Nassau County. It explores into the personal and professional challenges I faced, the inspiration I drew from the students, and the realities of working within a politically charged environment. Through it all, I learned valuable lessons about perseverance, the importance of following one's dreams, and the complexities of human nature.

Join me as I share my story of resilience, growth, and the unwavering belief that it's never too late to pursue your passions. Whether you are navigating your career, considering a major life transition, managing the pressures of office politics, or striving to balance personal and professional responsibilities, I hope my journey provides you with insights and encouragement to confidently forge your own path.

Chapter 1:
The Beginning

Introduction

Hello, and welcome to the beginning of my journey—a journey that has taken me from humble beginnings as a Public Safety Officer to my current role as an Instructor and Counselor at a local community college, in Nassau County. My name is Adeline Mucci, and I am excited to share my story with you.

Background

I immigrated to the United States in 1980 and graduated from Erasmus Hall High School in 1984. By 27, I had three children. After divorcing their father, I worked hard to ensure my children thrived in a single-parent household, relying on faith and determination.

My journey at a local community college, in Nassau County began over ten years ago when I joined the institution as a Public Safety Officer. As a member of the Public Safety team, my primary responsibility was to ensure the safety and security of students, faculty, and staff on campus. This encompassed a wide range of duties, including patrolling the campus grounds, responding to emergencies, enforcing campus policies, and providing assistance to individuals in need.

Each day brought new challenges and opportunities to serve the community. Whether it was assisting a lost student, diffusing a tense situation, or coordinating with local law enforcement agencies, no two days were ever the same. Despite the demanding nature of the job, I found fulfillment in knowing that I was making a tangible difference in the lives of those I served.

Inspiration

It was during my years as a Public Safety Officer that I found my greatest source of inspiration—the students of the local community college, in Nassau County. Interacting with students daily gave me unique insights into their lives, aspirations, and struggles. I was continually amazed by their resilience, determination, and commitment to their education.

Specific moments and encounters stand out in my memory, each leaving a profound impact on me. There was the first-generation college student who overcame immense obstacles to pursue his dream of higher education. His perseverance in the face of adversity inspired me to push beyond my own limitations and pursue further education.

Then there was the international student who navigated the complexities of a new culture and language with grace and courage. Her unwavering optimism and resilience in the face of challenges reminded me of the importance of embracing diversity and seizing every opportunity for growth. These are just a few examples of the countless moments and individuals who have inspired me along the way. Their stories, struggles, and triumphs have fueled my passion for education and instilled in me a deep sense of purpose.

The Unexpected Catalyst

One chilly morning, while on my usual patrol around the campus, I encountered a distraught young woman sitting alone on a bench. She was a freshman, overwhelmed by her new environment and struggling with homesickness. As I sat with her and listened to her fears, I realized how profoundly impactful of simply being present for someone in need. This moment was a turning point, planting the seed of my desire to transition into a more supportive role with students.

As I reflect on my early years at a local community college, in Nassau County, I am filled with gratitude for the experiences and opportunities that have shaped my journey. It is the students—their stories, their dreams, and their resilience—that continue to inspire me to strive for excellence and make a positive impact on the lives of others.

Chapter 2:
Academic Pursuit

Enrolling in a Master's Program

Deciding to enroll in a master's program was both exhilarating and daunting. After years of working as a Public Safety Officer, returning to academia represented a significant shift. I vividly remember the day I took the plunge. The students I interacted with daily sparked a desire in me to pursue further education — not only to better myself, but also to contribute more meaningfully to their lives.

The enrollment process was a journey in itself. I had to navigate various requirements: applications, transcripts, recommendation letters, and personal statements. This process starkly reminded me how long it had been since I had last applied to a school. I experienced moments of doubt and apprehension. Would I be able to keep up with the rigorous demands of a graduate program? Could I balance this new endeavor with my current job and personal responsibilities? These questions loomed large, but the desire to grow and to make a difference pushed me forward.

When I finally received the acceptance letter, it was a moment of triumph and validation. I was officially a graduate student, ready to embark on a new chapter in my life.

Juggling Roles

Balancing my role as a Public Safety Officer with that of a graduate student was a formidable challenge. My days were packed with responsibilities, and time management became an essential skill. My mornings and afternoons were spent patrolling the campus and ensuring the safety and security of students and staff. Evenings and weekends were dedicated to attending classes, completing assignments, and studying for exams.

The transition was far from seamless. There were countless late nights and early mornings, moments of exhaustion, and times when the workload felt overwhelming. However, I established a routine that allowed me to manage my duties effectively. I learned to prioritize tasks, delegate when possible, and make the most of every available moment. The discipline and structure I adopted during this period were crucial in helping me succeed both at work and in my studies.

One of the most significant factors in this juggling act was the support I received from my supervisors and colleagues. Understanding the importance of my academic pursuit, they often accommodated my schedule, allowing me to attend classes and study sessions. Their flexibility and encouragement were invaluable in helping me manage these dual responsibilities.

2001 Associate Degree

2012 Bachelor Degree

2019 Master Degree

My one and only son Mario

My youngest daughter Christina

My oldest daughter Marline

Support System

No journey of this magnitude is undertaken alone. Throughout my academic pursuit, I was fortunate to have a strong support system that played a crucial role in my success.

Family

My family was my rock during this time. Their unwavering belief in my abilities and their constant encouragement provided the emotional support I needed. They understood the demands on my time and were always there to lend a helping hand or a listening ear. Their presence reminded me that I was not alone in this journey, and their encouragement kept me motivated.

My Amazing Family

My Amazing Family

My Amazing Family

Conclusion

Enrolling in a master's program while working as a Public Safety Officer was a significant challenge, but it was also one of the most rewarding experiences of my life. The journey taught me the value of resilience, time management, and the importance of a strong support system. It reaffirmed my belief that it is never too late to pursue one's dreams and that with determination and support, we can overcome any obstacle.

Chapter 3:
The Role of Office Politics

Encountering Politics

Office politics can be a formidable force in any work environment, and my experiences at a local community college were no exception. I encountered various instances of office politics that tested my resolve and resilience. One

particular incident stands out — a moment that highlighted the subtle yet significant impact of office dynamics on individual careers.

About two years ago, as I transitioned from Public Safety Officer into my role as a Full-Time Instructor and Student Activities Counselor, I encountered resistance from a colleague who believed I was not polished enough for the position. Despite my qualifications and dedication to the role, their skepticism led to my transfer to another department. The experience was disheartening, to say the least. It felt like a setback — a judgment on my abilities and suitability for the position. However, instead of allowing it to deter me, I chose to view it as an opportunity for growth and introspection.

Navigating Restructuring

I firmly believe that every person we encounter in life offers us an opportunity for growth and self-discovery. This belief was reaffirmed during a pivotal experience I had at work. After being transferred to a different role within the same department, I observed the arrival of a new colleague — a talented and polished young woman who seemed to embody the qualities that had been deemed lacking in me by a former colleague.

Despite the initial challenges and feelings of uncertainty, we found ourselves collaborating as advisors for different clubs on campus. Together, we organized a series of successful events that garnered unprecedented attendance and student engagement. It was a testament to our collective efforts and dedication to fostering a vibrant campus community.

However, even with our achievements, the specter of office politics loomed large. Just as my new colleague was settling into her role, and with exemplary performance, she was informed that her position was being eliminated due to budget cuts. The timing and circumstances were bewildering, leaving me grappling with a profound sense of confusion and disillusionment.

A Harsh Reality

This experience underscored a harsh reality of the arbitrary nature of office politics, where merit and competence often take a backseat to personal biases and agendas. It became painfully clear that no amount of polish or professionalism could shield us from the capricious nature of workplace dynamics and their impact on individual careers in a workplace culture where personal preferences and alliances hold sway, and the dynamics of power, influence, and interpersonal relationships often play a significant role in shaping professional trajectories. It was a sobering reminder that merit and qualifications are not always the sole determinants of success. Despite our best efforts and contributions, we were both vulnerable to the whims of those in positions of power.

At first, I felt frustrated and disillusioned by the injustice of the situation. I questioned whether I belonged in the academic environment and whether my efforts would ever be recognized and valued. However, as time passed, I came to realize that dwelling on the negativity of the experience would only hold me back.

Instead, I chose to use the incident as a catalyst for personal and professional growth. I reflected on my strengths and weaknesses, identifying areas for improvement and development. I sought feedback from mentors and trusted colleagues, using their insights to refine my skills and to enhance my effectiveness in my role.

Chapter 4:
Lessons from a Colleague

Reflection on Experiences

This injustice for my colleague underscored the arbitrary nature of office politics and the often unpredictable professional landscape. Her grace and professionalism in handling this situation left a lasting impression on me. The experience poignantly reinforced the importance of resilience and perseverance in the face of adversity.

As I look back on both her experience and mine, I am grateful for the lessons they taught me. They strengthened my resolve, deepened my self-awareness, and reaffirmed my commitment to making a difference in the lives of students and colleagues. While office politics may continue to present challenges along the way, I am better equipped to navigate them with integrity and a dedicated focus on my goals.

Commitment to Fairness

While these experiences may have left me disheartened, they also reinforced my commitment to advocating for fairness and equity in the workplace. As I continue on my professional journey, I am determined to uphold these principles and to strive for a workplace culture where individuals are valued for their contributions, regardless of external perceptions or biases. I remain steadfast in my belief that despite our differences in style or approach, our intrinsic value as employees should not be contingent upon subjective opinions or superficial qualities, and that integrity, perseverance, and authenticity are the true markers of professional worth.

Conclusion

The incident with my colleague was a pivotal moment in my career — a reminder of the complexities of the professional world and the importance of staying true to oneself at all times. It served as a catalyst for personal and professional growth, propelling me forward on my journey of self-discovery and fulfillment. It taught me that setbacks are not indicators of failure, but opportunities for learning and growth. I refused to let one setback define my career trajectory, and, instead, I redoubled my efforts to prove my worth and to continue making a positive impact.

Chapter 5:
Personality vs Qualification

Navigating Competence vs. Bias

One of the most difficult challenges in the workplace arises when you are required to report to someone who lacks the competence to effectively lead. In such situations, your qualifications and expertise can become irrelevant, overshadowed by the personal biases of those in power. This behavior can foster a toxic workplace culture where newcomers are given little chance to succeed.

I have experienced instances where my qualifications were overlooked because of someone else's biases. It can be disheartening and frustrating, but I have learned to handle it by staying focused on my goals and by not letting others' opinions define my worth. I always try to use those moments as opportunities for growth and reflection, refining my skills and proving my value through my actions and achievements.

Instead of dwelling on unfairness, I channel my energy into becoming even better at what I do; and, whenever possible, I advocate for fairness and encourage a culture of meritocracy, ensuring that others do not have to face the same challenges.

Leading with integrity and fairness is crucial for fostering a positive and productive work environment. To ensure I embody these principles in my professional interactions, I focus on the following steps:

1. **Self-Reflection:** I regularly assess my own values and actions to ensure they align with the ethical standards I set for myself. This helps me stay true to my principles, even in challenging situations.
2. **Transparent Communication:** I prioritize clear, honest, and open communication with my team. This includes being upfront about decisions and the rationale behind them, which helps build trust and ensures everyone is on the same page.
3. **Active Listening:** I make it a point to listen to others' perspectives, especially when they differ from my own. This helps me understand the full context before making decisions, ensuring they are fair and consider all viewpoints.
4. **Consistency:** I strive to treat everyone equally and consistently, regardless of their position or my personal feelings. This means applying rules and standards uniformly and avoiding favoritism.
5. **Accountability:** I hold myself accountable for my actions and decisions. If I make a mistake, I acknowledge it, take corrective action, and learn from it. This sets a standard for others to follow and reinforces a culture of responsibility.

Chapter 6: Character is Destiny

Power of Character

"Character is destiny" encapsulates the idea that who we are at our core — our values, principles, and actions — ultimately shapes the course of our lives. It suggests that our character, more than external circumstances or luck, determines our fate. Our decisions, behaviors, and the way we respond to challenges are all reflections of our inner character, and these choices collectively steer the direction of our lives.

In the workplace, for example, a person of integrity who consistently acts with honesty and fairness is likely to earn the trust and respect of others, leading to opportunities for growth and leadership. On the other hand, someone who prioritizes short-term gains over ethical behavior may find success fleeting, as trust is eroded and relationships falter. In this way, character is not just a personal trait, but a powerful force that influences one's professional trajectory and long-term success.

On a broader level, the idea that "character is destiny" speaks to the impact we have on the world around us. Leaders who embody compassion, resilience, and integrity not only shape their own destinies, but also influence the futures of those they lead. Their character becomes a guiding light, setting the tone for the culture and values of their organizations. Conversely, leaders who lack strong character may create environments of fear, uncertainty, or unethical behavior, which can have lasting negative consequences.

Ultimately, "character is destiny" is a reminder that our true legacy is not defined by our achievements alone, but by the character we demonstrate in pursuing them. The adage challenges us to cultivate qualities like honesty, empathy, and perseverance, knowing that these will shape not only our own lives, but also the lives of those we touch. By adhering to these practices, I aim to create an environment where integrity and fairness are the foundation of all professional interactions.

Chapter 7: Lessons Learned

Personal Growth

Through the challenges and triumphs of my journey — from Public Safety Officer to Instructor and Counselor — I have experienced significant personal growth. Each obstacle I have faced, each moment of doubt and each success, has shaped me into the person I am today. Here are some of the key lessons I have learned:

- **Resilience:** Adversity is inevitable, but resilience is the key to overcoming it. I have learned to bounce back from setbacks, to persevere in the face of obstacles, and to remain steadfast in pursuing my goals.
- **Adaptability:** Change is constant, especially in the dynamic field of education. I have learned to embrace change, to be flexible in my approach, and to adapt to new circumstances and challenges.
- **Self-Reflection:** Personal growth requires self-awareness and introspection. I have learned to reflect on my experiences, to identify areas for improvement, and to continually strive for personal and professional development.

Professional Growth

In addition to personal growth, my journey has also been marked by significant professional growth. Here are some of the key lessons I have learned:

- **Collaboration:** The power of teamwork and collaboration cannot be overstated. I have learned that by working together with colleagues, we can achieve greater success and make a more significant impact.

- **Leadership:** Effective leadership requires empathy, integrity, and a commitment to fairness. I have learned to lead by example, to support and uplift others, and to advocate for a just and equitable workplace.

- **Student-Centered Approach:** At the heart of my role as an Instructor and Counselor is a commitment to students. I have learned to prioritize their needs, to listen to their voices, and to support their growth and development in every way possible.

Reflections on Office Politics

Office politics can be a challenging and often disheartening aspect of professional life. However, through my experiences, I have learned valuable lessons about navigating these dynamics:

- **Integrity:** Maintaining integrity and staying true to one's values is essential, even in the face of office politics. I have learned to remain honest, transparent, and ethical in my actions and decisions.

- **Resilience:** Office politics can be draining, but resilience is key to overcoming them. I have learned to stay focused on my goals, to persevere through challenges, and to remain undeterred by setbacks.

- **Advocacy:** Advocating for fairness and equity in the workplace is crucial. I have learned to speak up against injustice, to support my colleagues, and to strive for a workplace culture that values merit and integrity.

Chapter 8:
The Rewards of Perseverance

A Student's Letter

One of the most rewarding moments in my career came when I received a heartfelt letter from a former student. She expressed how my guidance and support had helped her navigate the challenges of college life and achieve her academic goals. This letter was a powerful reminder of the impact educators can have on their students' lives and reinforced my commitment to my role.

Unexpected recognition followed when I received an invitation from the Student Organization of Latinos (S.O.L.) on February 22, 2024. A colleague informed me that they were holding an event on March 7, 2024 at the local community college in Nassau County to honor Latinas who have contributed to the awareness of Latinx presence and contributions. I am the advisor of Haraya, a club that sponsors a variety of activities and events which focus on the African American experience and Africans in the diaspora. These programs, such as Kwanzaa and Black History Month, allow students to showcase their ideas and talents through speakers, conferences, trips, concerts, and more. Surprised and humbled that the students from the S.O.L. executive board remembered my contributions during our joint events, I was left speechless. Feeling appreciated is such a powerful thing. On the day of the event, I cried tears of joy, overwhelmed by the gratitude and acknowledgment.

Awards and Recognition

Receiving awards and recognition for my work is a humbling experience. These accolades are not just a testament to my efforts, but also a reflection of the support and encouragement I have received from my colleagues, students, and family. They serve as a reminder that perseverance and dedication do not go unnoticed.

For example, Haraya's Club hosted a Haitian Flag Day event on Tuesday, May 7, 2024. One of my colleagues invited a community leader to the event. She was so impressed with its success that she insisted on adding my name to the list of honorees for the Citation of Recognition at the Caribbean Heritage Month celebration scheduled for June 7, 2024 at Hempstead Town Hall. This event focused on countries like Cuba, Haiti, the Dominican Republic, Guyana, Jamaica, and Trinidad and Tobago. She felt strongly that I deserved to be recognized for my contributions based on what she had witnessed.

I could not have felt more proud that day as I received this award — a reminder that hard work truly pays off. I have always believed that whatever you do, you should do it with all your heart, and people will notice your efforts when you least expect it. Be patient, give 100% in everything you do, and the rewards will follow.

Conclusion

My journey from a Public Safety Officer to an Instructor and Counselor at a local community college in Nassau County has been filled with challenges, growth, and fulfillment. I have learned that it is never too late to pursue your dreams and that the support of loved ones is invaluable in overcoming obstacles. My experiences have shaped me into a more resilient and compassionate person, and I hope my story inspires others to follow their own paths with courage and determination.

Next Steps and Future Aspirations

As I continue my career in education, I am committed to furthering my professional development and exploring new ways to support my students. I plan to engage in research, attend conferences, and collaborate with colleagues to stay abreast of the latest trends and best practices in the field. My goal is to continuously improve and adapt to better serve the evolving needs of the student community.

I have also chosen to embrace gratitude and daily self-reflection, living life with thankfulness in all circumstances, recognizing that life's challenges happen to everyone. Life does not discriminate, and its lessons have only made me stronger and more resilient. When life hands me lemons, I make lemonade — and enjoy it with a fresh glass of ice. I have learned to turn insults into jokes and to understand that how we treat each other truly matters. Every person we encounter could be a potential customer or an important connection, and we risk missing out on opportunities if we get distracted by the "noise" around us.

Each day is a new opportunity to learn, grow, and make a difference in someone's life. By tuning out the distractions and focusing on what truly matters, we can contribute to a world that is better, happier, safer, and healthier. While I have earned my degree from the school of hard knocks, I know there are still a few lessons left for me to master.

Testimony #1 Celine Jean (2024)

1. **Impact on Academic Journey:** "You've given me unique advice that I wouldn't get from anyone else. You've inspired me to speak up, voice my opinions, and you've given me a newfound confidence that will serve me well in the future."

2. **Memorable Moment:** "When you asked about funding an event centered around Haitian culture, your passion for our heritage resonated with me. It made me proud to see another Haitian embracing our culture."

3. **Appreciated Qualities:** "Your warm and welcoming smile makes it easier to engage and listen, creating a positive learning environment."

4. **Support for Growth:** "Every conversation with you boosted my confidence and made me aspire to be as happy, consistent, and confident as you."

5. **Shaping Perspective:** "Interacting with you taught me that everyone's educational journey is unique. Comparing ourselves to others is unfair; we all have different paths to different goals."

6. **Lasting Advice:** "Your story of pursuing education instead of settling at your previous job was really admirable. It gave me a lot of support in my own journey."

7. **Recommendation:** "If you want someone who will uplift you, give you confidence, and show you what dedication is, you're the right counselor for them."

Testimony #2 - Destany Samuel (2023)

1. **Impact on Academic Journey:** "You didn't just teach me; you guided me through the most challenging parts of my academic journey. Your support and encouragement were pivotal in shaping my academic success."

2. **Memorable Moment:** "Your personal journey of overcoming obstacles to get your master's degree taught me the power of perseverance and resilience. It inspires me whenever I face challenges."

3. **Appreciated Qualities:** "I appreciate your genuine care and compassion. You listen without judgment and offer tailored advice, making me feel valued and supported."

4. **Support for Growth:** "You consistently encouraged me to reach for the stars and beyond, celebrating my accomplishments as if they were your own. That means the world to me!"
5. **Shaping Perspective:** "You've taught me that education is a lifelong journey, and there are good people who genuinely care about the positive progression of their students."
6. **Lasting Advice:** "You taught me that life is all about learning from one another and creating a safe space for community and different perspectives. This simple yet powerful message has become my mantra."
7. **Recommendation:** "You're more than just a teacher; you're a guide, a mentor, and a friend. Your role in my college experience has been invaluable, and I wouldn't be where I am today without your unwavering support."

Testimony #3 - Godlee Sainvilus (2022)

1. **Impact on Academic Journey:** "You encouraged me to improve my grades when I had lost faith in myself. Your support was a big reason why I improved."

2. **Memorable Moment:** "When you noticed that I needed to hear that I was smart too, it reminded me that I am a bright person with my own unique qualities."

3. **Appreciated Qualities:** "You're very personal, creating a safe space for people to share and feel loved and listened to."

4. **Support for Growth:** "Whether it was a quick hello or advice, you always had something

inspirational to say, which I could apply to my life."

5. **Shaping Perspective:** "You ignited a light of hope and confidence in me. Your belief in me helped me believe in myself again, and I am eternally grateful."

6. **Lasting Advice:** "You reminded me that I know what's best for me and not to let anyone get in the way of my vision."

7. **Recommendation:** "I'd tell future students that clear communication is key. Working with you taught me the importance of staying on the same page and understanding what is needed."

Testimony #4 - Kalayah Johnson (2022)

1. **Impact on Academic Journey:** "Prof. Mucci has been a huge inspiration and driving force in my academic journey. As my club advisor, she encouraged us to host activities and pursue our academic goals."

2. **Memorable Moment:** "When I was 1 credit short of graduation, Prof. Mucci worked with me to remedy the situation. Her assistance and encouragement helped me graduate on time."

3. **Appreciated Qualities:** "Every interaction with Prof. Mucci feels like talking to family. She has an overwhelmingly optimistic approach that's infectious."

4. **Support for Growth:** "Prof. Mucci played a vital role in the completion of my degree and supported our club activities, demonstrating diligence and thorough planning."

5. **Shaping Perspective:** "Our interactions have left me excited to tackle my future career goals, knowing that small steps toward my vision are incredibly valuable."

6. **Lasting Advice:** "One piece of advice that will last far beyond my years working with Prof. Mucci is that perseverance is a powerful tool most people lack. Always work towards your goals, even when they seem unattainable."

7. **Recommendation:** "Working with Prof. Mucci provides a prime example of diligence and perseverance. She helps students elevate themselves to a higher standard."

Testimony #5 - Christopher August (2022)

1. **Impact on Academic Journey:** "Having you as my instructor has changed the way I approach my studies. You've become a huge source of inspiration, motivating me to aim higher every day."

2. **Memorable Moment:** "When you told me to 'meet your brother where he's at,' it taught me patience and acceptance, which changed how I handle challenges."

3. **Appreciated Qualities:** "Your kindness, motivation, and genuine care make each of us feel important. Your support goes beyond academics, which I really appreciate."

4. **Support for Growth:** "Learning to meet people where they're at has helped me handle

relationships and conflicts, allowing me to stay focused on what really matters."

5. **Shaping Perspective:** "Your encouragement has helped me dream bigger and work harder toward my goals, reminding me that I can achieve anything I set my mind to."

6. **Lasting Advice:** "You reminded me that it's okay to make mistakes because life is about learning from them. This perspective has helped me keep going, knowing that setbacks are just part of the journey."

7. **Recommendation:** "You're the heart of the local community college in Nassau County. Thanks to you, my college experience has been amazing. You've made a big impact on my life, both as a professor and a counselor, and I'm so grateful for your support."

Testimony #6- Isaac Zellner (2024)

1. **Impact on Academic Journey:** First, I want to say how honored and grateful I am to have had the privilege of learning from this phenomenal woman! Your knowledge and wisdom have been instrumental in helping me shape and achieve my academic and personal goals.

2. **Memorable Moment:** The first time we met was a particularly special moment for me. Your encouragement and wise words about staying determined, focused, and on the right path despite distractions were truly inspiring. You assured me that I would succeed not only in my academics but also in life. You told me I am a star and that you could see me on Broadway and

in big-time shows. You didn't just speak these words—you acted on them by investing your time and resources to ensure I was prepared for my fall 2024 semester classes. For your support and belief in me, I am deeply grateful.

3. **How did it influence you?:** Ms. Adeline, your personality and character have had a profound influence on me. You've shown me that anything I set my mind to is within my reach, and I'm now more confident in my ability to achieve greatness.

4. **Appreciated Qualities:** You embody greatness in every sense. You are a woman of virtue, with a foundation built on integrity, grace, dignity, poise, class, faith, structure, order, humanity, humility, and determination.

5. **Support for Growth:** As I mentioned before, it's your character and who you are that have made the difference. You ensured I was fully prepared for a successful semester. Through your influence, knowledge, wisdom, and valuable resources, you helped me not only successfully withdraw from last semester but also present a pending refund case to the President's Committee. This support has significantly impacted my academic career, setting me up for future success both professionally and personally.

6. **Shaping Perspective:** Our first interaction was transformative, shaping my perspective on both my education and future. Ms. Adeline, you

reminded me that my purpose, destiny, and the plans GOD has for me are not just for my benefit—they're meant to touch and affect others as well. This realization is truly a divine connection.

7. **Lasting Advice:** The advice that has left the deepest impression on me is your constant encouragement to keep going, keep achieving, and most importantly, to keep seeking GOD.

8. **Recommendation:** This woman of greatness is more than just a counselor or academic advisor. She not only aids students but also propels them into their destiny and purpose—especially those who are truly committed to their own growth and success.

Testimony #7- Nathan Cheong (2023)

1. **Impact on Academic Journey**: Ms. Adeline, as a counselor, has been one of the most positive influences in my life. She has always been a consistent reminder that God is always good, and through Him, all things are possible. Her encouraging approach to life has inspired me to make the necessary decisions to pursue my dreams.

2. **Memorable Moment**: One of my favorite moments was when a friend, Coralie, and I were in the lobby of the CCB at Nassau Community College. Ms. Adeline was there, describing her ongoing journey and emphasizing that in life, it's important to crawl before you can walk.

3. **Appreciated Qualities**: This encounter reminded me to stay humble and make every moment count. By focusing on the next step, you won't fall far from where you're trying to go.

4. **Support for Growth**: What I appreciate most is her unfiltered honesty.

5. **Shaping Perspective**: The way I approach life has been influenced by Ms. Adeline. I try to carry joy with me at all times, through both hardships and ease.

6. **Lasting Advice**: The advice that has stayed with me is that if we aim too high, we can fall too far. So, dream big, but focus on each step.

7. **Recommendation**: There isn't anyone who understands better the work needed to move forward in life amidst pressure.

Testimony #8- Olga Komarnicki (Kosovskikh) (2016)

1. **Impact on Academic Journey:** "You helped me with learning English, which allowed me to pursue my other goals in life. Your instruction improved my grammar, enabling me to express my thoughts more clearly in my college studies and in my personal and professional life."

2. **Memorable Moment:** "I remember when we discussed the future and the importance of having a goal to be successful and to be thankful for what has happened in my life. This influenced me to continue working towards my goal even when loved ones faced health emergencies."

3. **Appreciated Qualities:** "I appreciate how you help all students, no matter their background. Your ability to communicate, your patience, and your command of multiple languages were especially inspiring."

4. **Support for Growth:** "You supported my personal growth by setting an example of how to listen and be patient with people. When dealing with individuals who speak a different primary language, I often get frustrated when I can't convey my thoughts quickly or understand the other person. Following your example, I've made great improvements."

5. **Shaping Perspective:** "Your help kept me from quitting or delaying my education due to the language difficulties I experienced as a non-native English speaker."

6. **Lasting Advice:** "Because of your advice and guidance, I never gave up on my dreams or stopped working towards my future."

7. **Recommendation:** "I would tell future students that you are patient and always willing to put in the extra time to help them understand the lesson or their expectations."

Final Thought:

These testimonies reflect the profound impact I've had on my students, both academically and personally. They highlight my dedication, encouragement, and the unique qualities that make me an exceptional instructor and counselor. The indescribable joy of witnessing a graduated student return to our local community college in Nassau County solely to express their gratitude for the role we played in their achievement is a moment I cherish deeply. For faculty members, this is the pinnacle of fulfillment—the most rewarding experience we could hope for.

As we journey through life, it's crucial to make a difference every day and be intentional in our actions. Share your struggles with others, and you'll find that we are all more connected than we realize. Don't stand on the sidelines, constantly complaining; instead, find solutions to the problems you face. Encourage your hearts, unite in love, and be relentless in your pursuit of growth and connection.

We come from different ages, backgrounds, and walks of life, but love and passion should guide us to support one another through life's challenges. There's a saying that goes, "A regular teacher just tells us things, a good teacher explains them, a better teacher shows us how, but a great teacher inspires us." Strive to do what others won't, to make a difference in someone else's life. We were not meant to live and struggle alone; we can only win when we unite, bringing victory to us all.

A title alone does not define leadership; true leadership is measured by the impact and influence one has. When people ask me the difference between a boss and a leader, my answer is simple: a boss holds a title, but a leader earns the trust of their people. I believe it's possible to be both, but it requires self-improvement and a focus on what truly matters to help the organization thrive.

Thank you for joining me on this journey. I hope that my experiences and lessons resonate with you and inspire you to navigate your path with courage, perseverance, and authenticity. Remember, every challenge is an opportunity for growth, and every setback is a stepping stone toward success.

Receiving an Award of Recognition from the Town of Hempstead

Birthday Celebration with My Students

Friendsgiving Celebration with My Students

Celebrating Art with a Talented Student

Spring Fest 2024 Celebration

The joy of meeting a new student who shares my name.

www.ingramcontent.com/pod-product-compliance
Lightning Source LLC
LaVergne TN
LVHW022001060526
838201LV00048B/1648